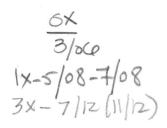

6X
———
3/06

1x-5/08-7/08
3x- 7/12 (11/12)

OB

D0633626

SPIDER

Life Cycles

Jason Cooper

Rourke

Publishing LLC
Vero Beach, Florida 32964

www.rourkepublishing.com

PHOTO CREDITS:
Cover, pp. 4, 6, 8, 16, 22 (stage 4) © Lynn M. Stone; pp. 7, 10, 12, 13, 14, 18, 19, 20, 22 (stages 1, 2, and 3) © James H. Carmichael

Editor: Frank Sloan

Cover and page design by Nicola Stratford

Library of Congress Cataloging-in-Publication Data

Cooper, Jason

ISBN 1-58952-707-0

Printed in the USA

CG/CG

Table of Contents

This fishing spider is on the surface of a Florida pond.

Spiders

Spiders are everywhere. They can be found in deserts, forests, ponds, prairies, and—yes—in homes. There aren't too many places without spiders of one **species** or another. And there are plenty of species! Scientists know of some 30,000 species of spiders. It is likely they'll find another 30,000.

Some spiders leap. Some fish. Some set ambushes for their **prey**. Some spin beautiful webs. And all of them produce threads of silk.

The first thing to know about spiders is that they are not insects. Like insects, spiders are boneless and **cold-blooded**. But spiders belong to a group of animals called **arachnids**.

This garden spider must warm in the early morning sun before it can move about.

Jumping spiders leap to capture their prey.

Spiders and other arachnids have eight legs. Insects have six. Most insects have wings and antennas. Spiders have neither.

The common garden spider uses silk both to spin a web and later wrap its prey.

Spiders are different than other arachnids, such as horseshoe crabs, because they make silk. Silk is stored as a liquid in a spider. When the spider releases silk, it dries into an extremely thin, but strong, thread. Spiders never go anywhere without leaving a line of silk behind. The silk is a lifeline the spider can climb.

A female red-legged widow guards three egg sacs in her web.

From Egg to Adult

A spider begins life inside a tiny egg. A female spider may lay 100 eggs, or she may lay 2,000. How many eggs she lays depends upon the kind of spider.

Most kinds of spiders put their eggs in a silk-wrapped pouch, or **sac**. Some kinds of spiders die after making the egg sac. Other kinds stay with the sac and guard it. Certain spiders carry the sac around with them!

Baby spiders, or spiderlings, hatch inside the sac. The sac is a nursery web for the spiderlings. Inside the sac, the spiderlings **molt**.

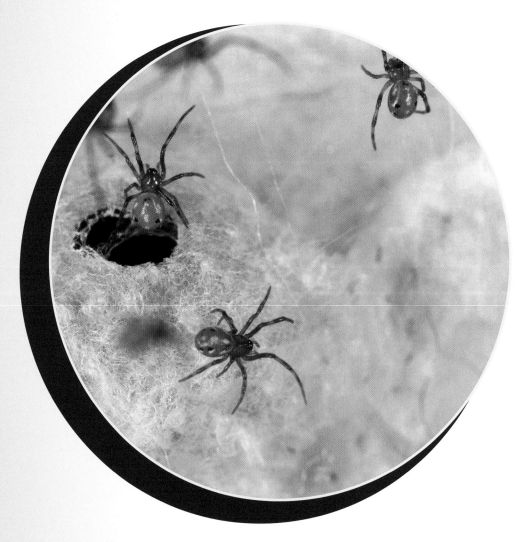

Red-legged widow spiderlings leave their egg sac.

Wolf spider babies ride on the back of their mother.

A molt is a change of skins. As a spiderling's body begins to grow, its tough skin doesn't grow with it. The old covering, called a cast, splits open. The spider crawls out, leaving the first skin behind like an old coat. A new skin forms.

A golden silk spider rides a thread of silk down from the old skin it has left behind.

After the first molt, spiderlings leave the nursery. After leaving, some kinds of spiderlings are on their own. In some species, spiderlings climb on their mother's back. Other kinds remain with their mother in a burrow or web. In many species, the mother spider shares food with her young for as many as two or three years!

As young spiders grow, they continue to molt. Most species molt five to nine times. The big, hairy spiders called tarantulas may molt 20 times.

As spiders go, tarantulas are large.

The Lives of Spiders

Sooner or later, a young spider lives on its own. Few kinds of spiders live in spider groups.

For a spider, growing up doesn't mean growing large. The smallest spiders are the size of pin heads. Even the largest tarantulas are no more than 10 inches (25 centimeters) across from leg to leg.

Female spiders are usually larger than males. Male spiders can be in danger when they approach a female. The male must quickly show **courtship** behavior. It must show it likes the female and means no harm. Otherwise, the male may be attacked by the lady it wanted for a mate!

The female red-legged widow (left) guards her egg sac while a much smaller male carefully comes near.

A crab spider, here with a bee, hunts from ambush.

Spiders are **predators**. They hunt other little animals. Some species, about one in ten, catch prey in a silk web. Others hunt from a hiding place or jump upon their prey. Spitting spiders shoot a silk net over their prey.

The fishing spider will eat this minnow it has caught.

Most spiders eat insects. A web, for example, may catch 500 or more insects each day. But some spiders catch fish, other spiders, or even mice and small birds. In turn, spiders are prey for larger animals, such as birds, snakes, and larger spiders.

Spiders kill their prey with fangs and **venom**. But to people, spiders are far more interesting than they are dangerous.

Stage 1:
Spiders begin life
in an egg

Stage 4:
An adult spider can start
a new cycle of
life for its species

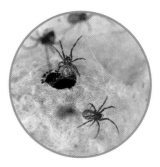

Stage 2:
Spiderlings hatch
from eggs

Stage 3:
Spiders grow by
leaving their old,
outer skins behind

Glossary

arachnids (uh RACK nidz) — small, boneless, cold-blooded animals including such animals as spiders, ticks, mites, and horseshoe crabs

cold-blooded (KOLD BLUHD ed) — refers to animals whose body temperature changes with the climate

courtship (KORT SHIP) — certain behavior that happens when one animal tries to win the attention of another

molt (MOLT) — to undergo a change in covering, such as a new shell replacing an old

predators (PRED uht urz) — animals that kill other animals for food

prey (PRAY) — an animal that is hunted for food by another animal

sac (SACK) — a pouch in which eggs may be laid or carried

species (SPEE sheez) — within a group of closely related animals, one certain kind, such as a lynx spider

venom (VEN um) — poison

Index

Further Reading

Greenberg, Daniel A. *Spiders.* Marshall Cavendish, 2001

Kallen, Stuart A. *Spiders.* Kidhaven Press, 2001

Schaefer, Lola M. *Spiders: Spinners and Trappers.* Bridgestone, 2002

Steele, Christy. *Tarantulas.* Steadwell Books, 2001

Websites to Visit

www.nhaudubon.org/naturalist/naturalistspider.htm
www.phs.org/saf/transcripts/transcript905.htm

About the Author

Jason Cooper has written several children's books about a variety of topics for Rourke Publishing, including the recent series *Life Cycles* and *Fighting Forces.* Cooper travels widely to gather information for his books.